My City

Jan Pritchett

Rigby®
A Harcourt Achieve Imprint

www.Rigby.com
1-800-531-5015

This is the airport in the daytime.

This is the airport at night.

This is a street in the daytime.

4

This is a street at night.

This is our library in the daytime.

This is our library at night.

This is the grocery store
in the daytime.

This is the grocery store
at night.

This is the flower store
in the daytime.

This is the flower store
at night.

This is our playground
in the daytime.

This is our playground
at night.

This is my house in the daytime.

This is my house at night.

This is my city.